HAL LEONARD
STUDENT
PIANO
LIBRARY

More Christmas Piano Solos

For All Piano Methods

D0504035

Table of Contents

Book: ISBN 978-1-4234-8361-8
Book/CD: ISBN 978-1-4234-9326-6

HAL•LEONARD®
CORPORATION
7777 W. BLUEMOUND RD. P.O. BOX 13819 MILWAUKEE, WI 53213

For all works contained herein:
Unauthorized copying, arranging, adapting, recording, Internet posting, public performance,
or other distribution of the printed or recorded music in this publication is an infringement of copyright.
Infringers are liable under the law.

Visit Hal Leonard Online at
www.halleonard.com

Here Comes Santa Claus
(Right Down Santa Claus Lane)

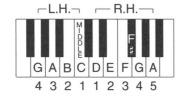

Words and Music by Gene Autry
and Oakley Haldeman
Arranged by Fred Kern

Moderately

Here comes Santa Claus! | Here comes Santa Claus! | Right down Santa Claus | Lane!

Accompaniment (Student plays one octave higher than written.) 🔘 **TRACKS** 1/2

Moderately (♩ = 120)

© 1947 (Renewed) Gene Autry's Western Music Publishing Co.
This arrangement © 2009 (Renewed) Gene Autry's Western Music Publishing Co.
All Rights Reserved   Used by Permission

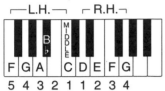

Frosty the Snow Man

Words and Music by
Steve Nelson and Jack Rollins
Arranged by Mona Rejino

With spirit; in "two"

Fros - ty the Snow Man _____ was a
Fros - ty the Snow Man _____ is a

jol - ly, hap - py soul _____ with a
fair - y tale, they say; _____ he was

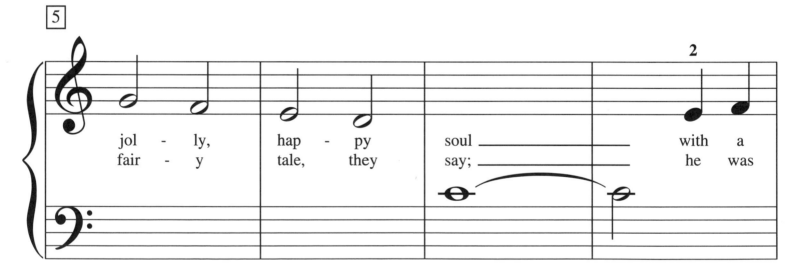

Accompaniment (Student plays one octave higher than written.)

TRACKS
3/4

With spirit, in "two" (♩ = 120)

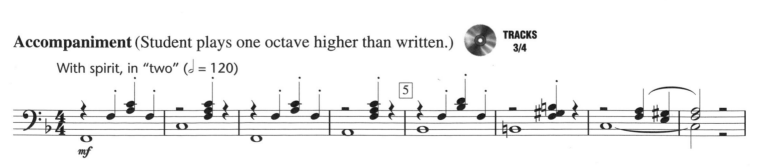

Copyright © 1950 by Chappell & Co.
Copyright Renewed
This arrangement Copyright © 2009 by Chappell & Co.
International Copyright Secured   All Rights Reserved

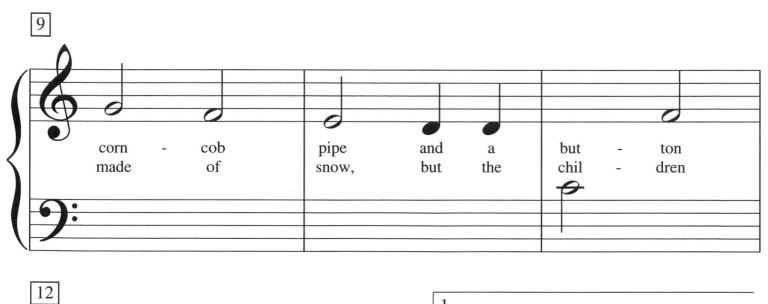

corn - cob pipe and a but - ton
made of snow, but the chil - dren

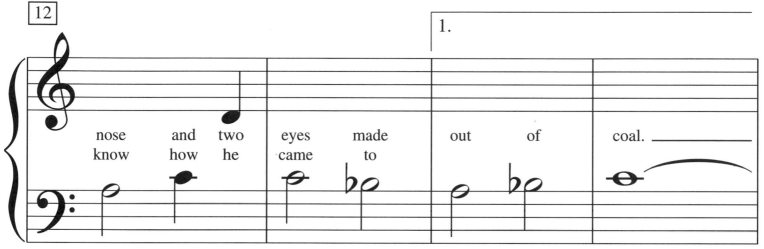

1.

nose and two eyes made out of coal. _____
know how he came to

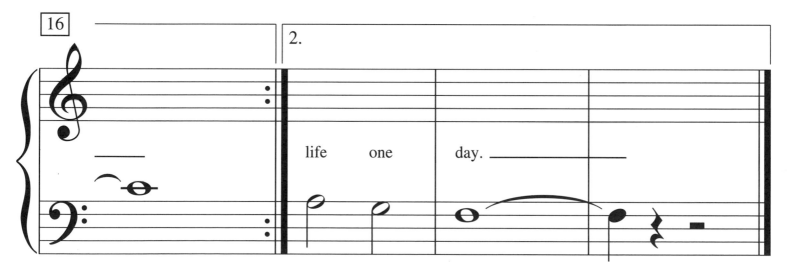

2.

life one day. _____

5

The Snow Lay on the Ground

Traditional Irish Carol
Arranged by Mona Rejino

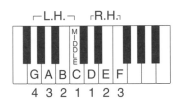

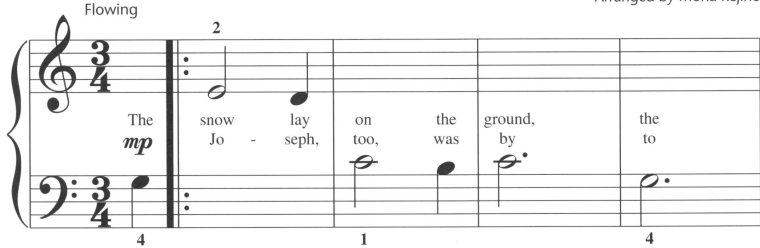

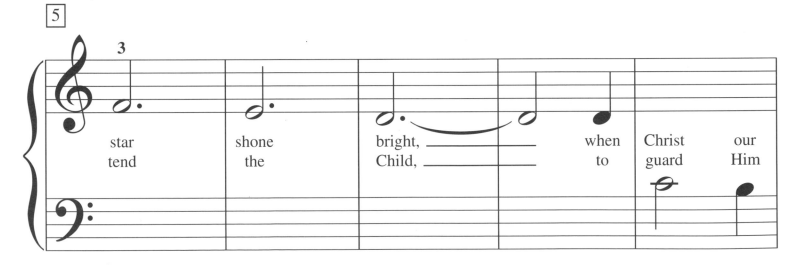

Accompaniment (Student plays one octave higher than written.) TRACKS 5/6

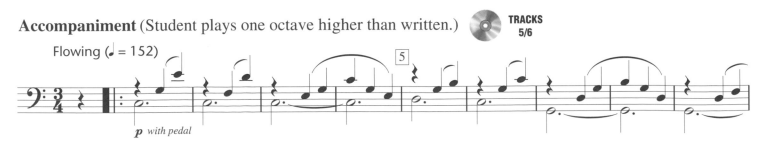

Copyright © 2009 by HAL LEONARD CORPORATION
International Copyright Secured   All Rights Reserved

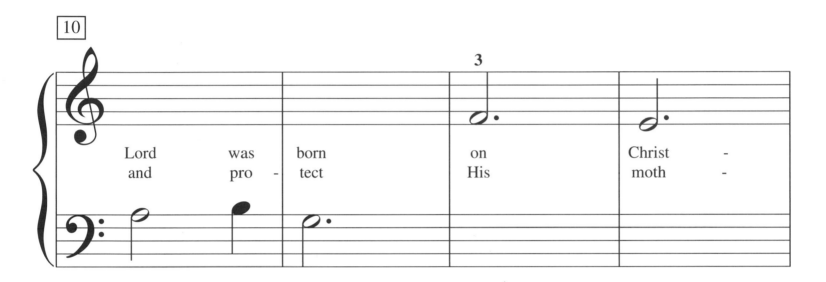

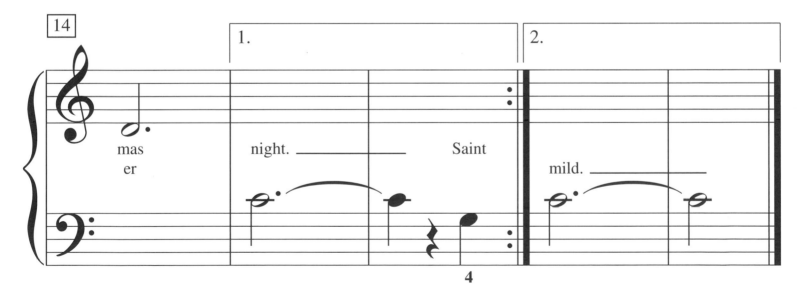

Joy to the World

Words by Isaac Watts
Music by George Frideric Handel
Adapted by Lowell Mason
Arranged by Phillip Keveren

Accompaniment (Student plays one octave higher than written.) 🔘 **TRACKS** 7/8

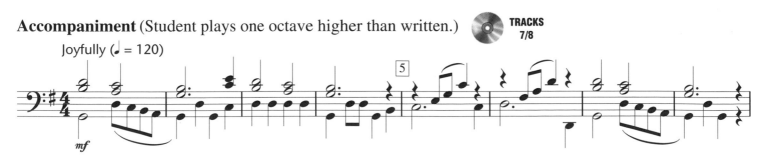

Copyright © 2009 by HAL LEONARD CORPORATION
International Copyright Secured   All Rights Reserved

Over the River
and Through the Woods

Traditional
Arranged by Carol Klose

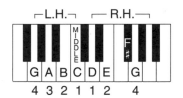

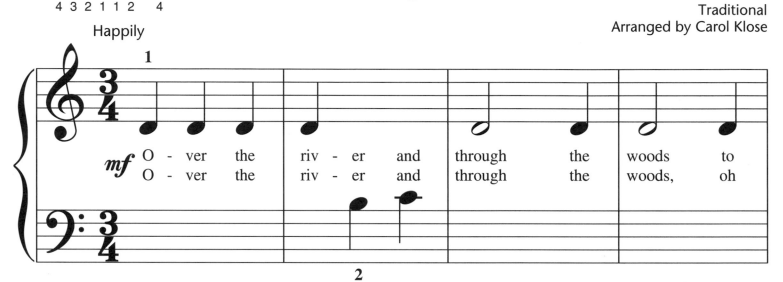

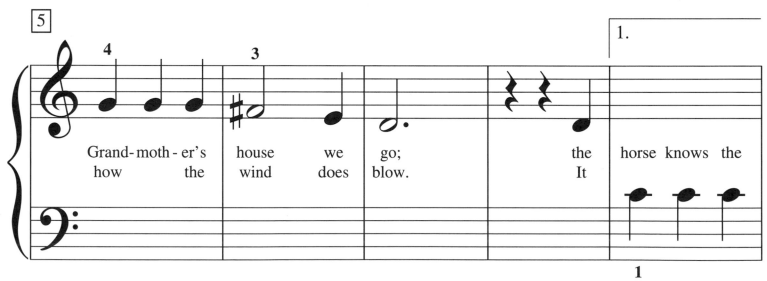

Accompaniment (Student plays one octave higher than written.)

TRACKS 9/10

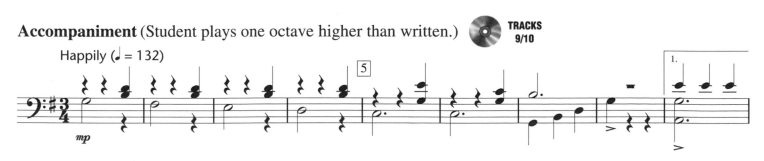

Copyright © 2009 by HAL LEONARD CORPORATION
International Copyright Secured All Rights Reserved

Do You Hear What I Hear

Words and Music by Noel Regney
and Gloria Shayne
Arranged by Phillip Keveren

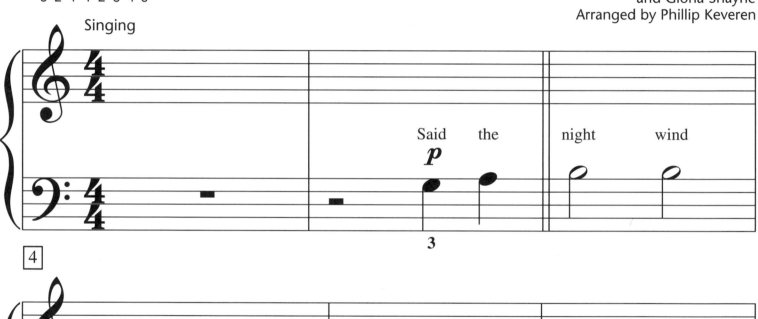

Singing

Said the p night wind

3

4

to the lit-tle lamb: _____

Accompaniment (Student plays one octave higher than written.) **TRACKS 11/12**

Singing ($\frac{1}{2}$ = 63)

pp

Copyright © 1962 (Renewed) by Jewel Music Publishing Co., Inc. (ASCAP)
This arrangement Copyright © 2009 by Jewel Music Publishing Co., Inc. (ASCAP)
International Copyright Secured   All Rights Reserved
Used by Permission

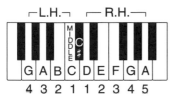

Blue Christmas

Words and Music by Billy Hayes
and Jay Johnson
Arranged by Fred Kern

With expression

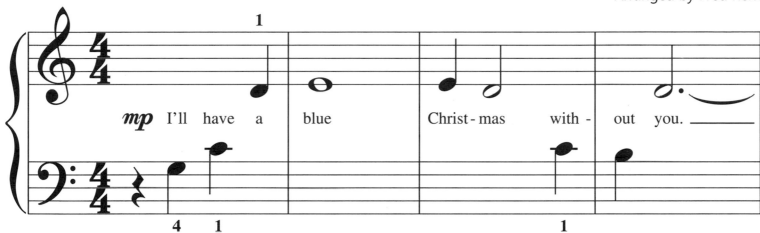

mp I'll have a blue Christ-mas with - out you. ____

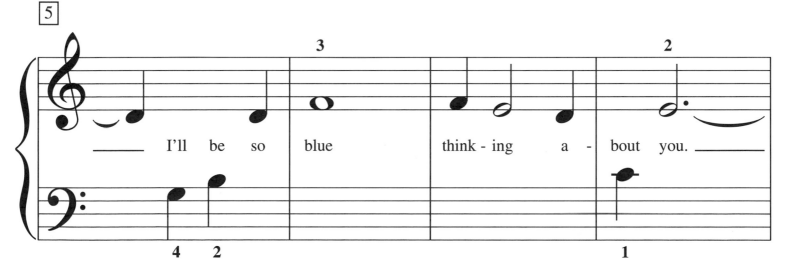

____ I'll be so blue think - ing a - bout you. ____

Accompaniment (Student plays one octave higher than written.)

TRACKS
13/14

With expression (♩ = 120)

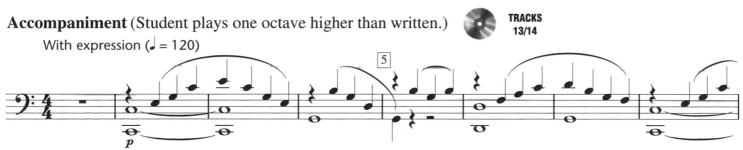

Copyright © 1948 UNIVERSAL - POLYGRAM INTERNATIONAL PUBLISHING, INC.
Copyright Renewed
This arrangement Copyright © 2009 UNIVERSAL - POLYGRAM INTERNATIONAL PUBLISHING, INC.
All Rights Reserved   Used by Permission

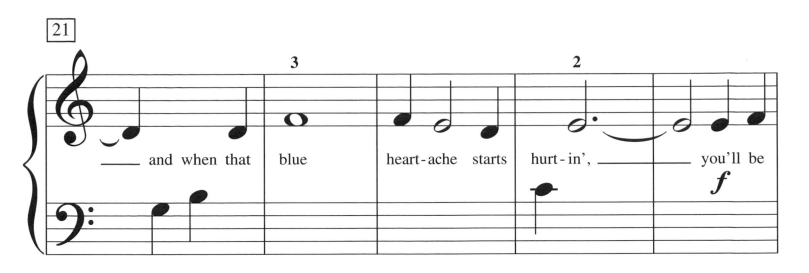

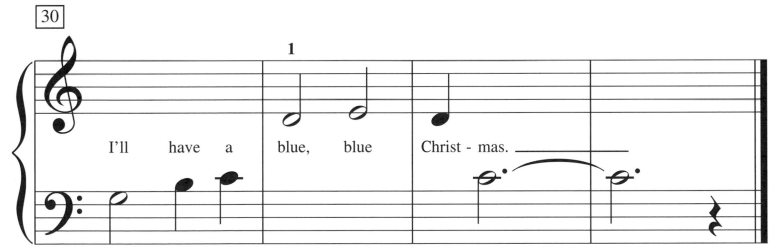

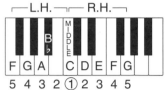

Rudolph the Red-Nosed Reindeer

Music and Lyrics by Johnny Marks
Arranged by Jennifer Linn

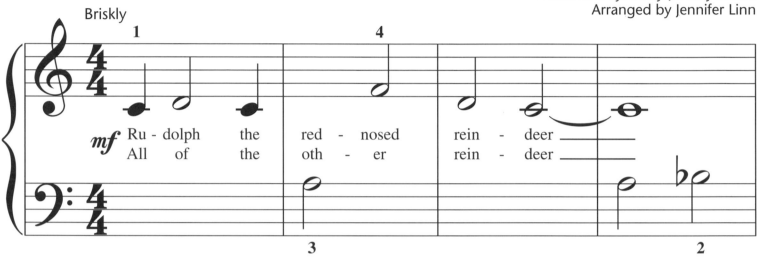

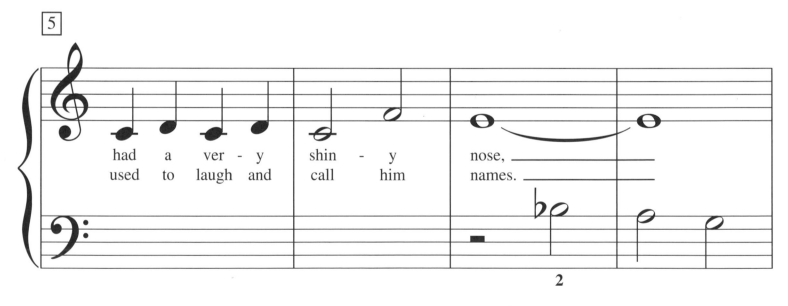

Accompaniment (Student plays one octave higher than written.) **TRACKS 15/16**

Briskly (♩ = 108)

Copyright © 1949 (Renewed 1977) St. Nicholas Music Inc., 1619 Broadway, New York, New York 10019
This arrangement Copyright © 2009 St. Nicholas Music Inc.
All Rights Reserved

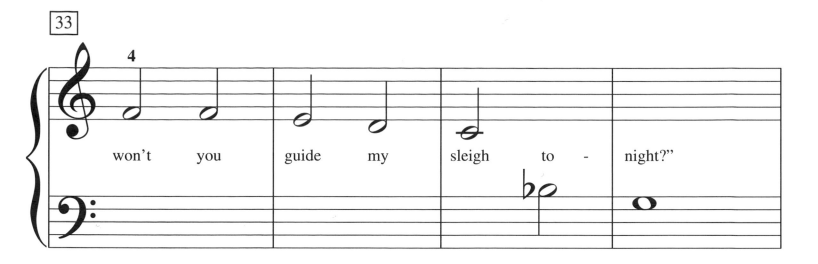

won't   you   guide   my   sleigh   to -   night?"

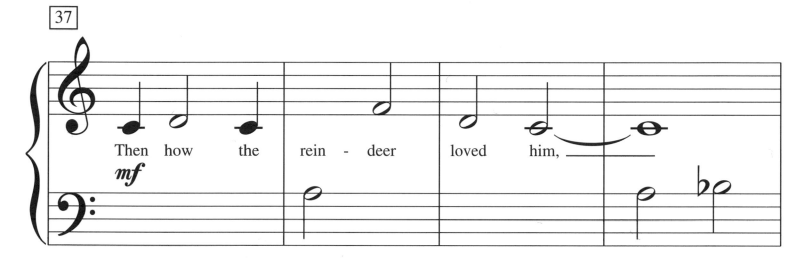

Then how   the   rein - deer   loved   him, _____

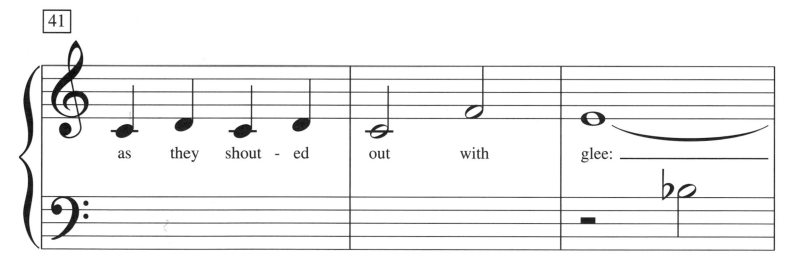

as   they   shout - ed   out   with   glee: _____

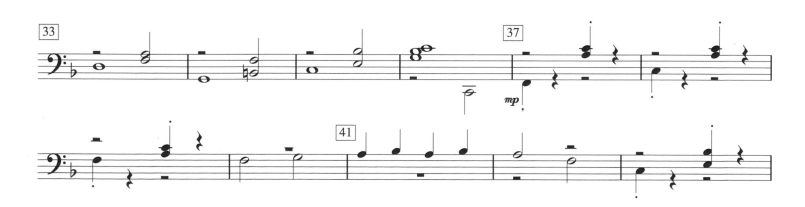

CELEBRATE THE HOLIDAYS WITH THE
HAL LEONARD STUDENT PIANO LIBRARY

Christmas Piano Solos

Favorite carols and seasonal songs, many with great teacher accompaniments! Instrumental accompaniments are also available on CD and GM disk. Arranged by Fred Kern, Phillip Keveren, Mona Rejino and Bruce Berr.

Level 1
00296049	Book Only	$6.99
00296081	CD Only	$10.95
00296101	GM Disk Only	$12.95

Level 2
00296050	Book Only	$6.99
00296082	CD Only	$10.95
00296102	GM Disk Only	$12.95

Level 3
00296051	Book Only	$6.95
00296083	CD Only	$10.95
00296103	GM Disk Only	$12.95

Level 4
00296052	Book Only	$6.95
00296084	CD Only	$10.95
00296104	GM Disk Only	$12.95

Level 5
00296146	Book Only	$6.95
00296159	CD Only	$10.95
00296162	GM Disk Only	$12.95

Christmas Piano Ensembles

Four-part student ensembles arranged for two or more pianos by Phillip Keveren. Featuring favorite Christmas carols and hymns in graded books that correspond directly to the five levels of the Hal Leonard Student Piano Library. CD and GM disk accompaniments are available separately.

Level 1
00296338	Book Only	$6.95
00296343	CD Only	$10.95
00296348	GM Disk Only	$12.95

Level 2
00296339	Book Only	$6.95
00296344	CD Only	$10.95
00296349	GM Disk Only	$12.95

Level 3
00296340	Book Only	$6.95
00296345	CD Only	$10.95
00296350	GM Disk Only	$12.95

Level 4
00296341	Book Only	$6.95
00296346	CD Only	$10.95
00296351	GM Disk Only	$12.95

Level 5
00296342	Book Only	$6.95
00296347	CD Only	$10.95
00296352	GM Disk Only	$12.95

More Christmas Piano Solos

Following up on the success of the Christmas Piano Solos books for levels 1-5 in the Hal Leonard Student Piano Library, these books contain additional holiday selections for each grade level that will work great with any piano method. Each song includes an optional teacher accompaniment. Arranged by Fred Kern, Phillip Keveren, Carol Klose, Jennifer Linn and Mona Rejino.

Pre-Staff
00296790	Book Only	$6.99

Level 1
00296791	Book Only	$6.99

Level 2
00296792	Book Only	$6.99

Level 3
00296793	Book Only	$6.99

Level 4
00296794	Book Only	$7.99

Level 5
00296795	Book Only	$7.99

Festive Chanukah Songs – Level 2
arranged by Bruce Berr

7 solos with teacher accompaniments: Candle Blessings • Chanukah • Come Light The Menorah • Hanérot, Halalu • The Dreydl Song • S'vivon • Ma'oz Tsur.

00296194 .... $5.95

Festive Songs for the Jewish Holidays – Level 3
arranged by Bruce Berr

11 solos, some with teacher accompaniments: Who Can Retell? • Come Light The Menorah • S'vivon • Ma'oz Tsur • I Have A Little Dreydl • Dayénu • Adir Hu • Eliyahu Hanavi • Chad Gadya • Hatikvah.

00296195... $6.99

FOR MORE INFORMATION, SEE YOUR LOCAL MUSIC DEALER,
OR WRITE TO:

HAL•LEONARD® CORPORATION
7777 W. BLUEMOUND RD. P.O. BOX 13819 MILWAUKEE, WI 53213

www.halleonard.com

Prices, contents, and availability subject to change without notice. Some products may not be available outside the U.S.A.

0709